POETRY MONSTERS

Scotland

Edited By Sarah Olivo

First published in Great Britain in 2019 by:

Young Writers Est. 1991

Young Writers
Remus House
Coltsfoot Drive
Peterborough
PE2 9BF
Telephone: 01733 890066
Website: www.youngwriters.co.uk

Book Design by Ashley Janson

Softback ISBN 978-1-83928-558-5

Printed and bound in the UK by BookPrintingUK
Website: www.bookprintinguk.com
YB0426E

FOREWORD

Hello Reader!

For our latest poetry competition we sent out funky and vibrant worksheets for primary school pupils to fill in and create their very own poem about fiendish fiends and crazy creatures. I got to read them and guess what? They were **roarsome**!

The pupils were able to read our example poems and use the fun-filled free resources to help bring their imaginations to life, and the result is pages **oozing** with exciting poetic tales. From friendly monsters to mean monsters, from bumps in the night to **rip-roaring** adventures, these pupils have excelled themselves, and now have the joy of seeing their work in print!

Here at Young Writers we love nothing more than poetry and creativity. We aim to encourage children to put pen to paper to inspire a love of the written word and explore their own unique worlds of creativity. We'd like to congratulate all of the aspiring authors that have created this book of **monstrous mayhem** and we know that these poems will be enjoyed for years to come. So, dive on in and submerge yourself in all things furry and fearsome (and perhaps check under the bed!).

CONTENTS

Our Lady Of Loretto Primary School, Dalmuir

Ratho Primary School, Ratho

Thorn Primary School, Johnstone

Townhill Primary School, Townhill

Turriff Primary School, Turriff

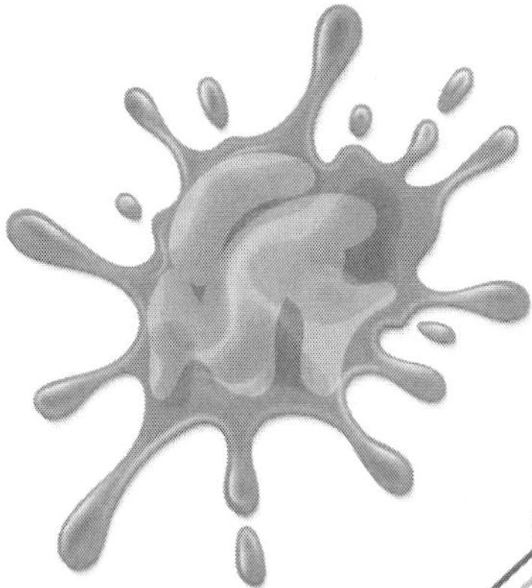

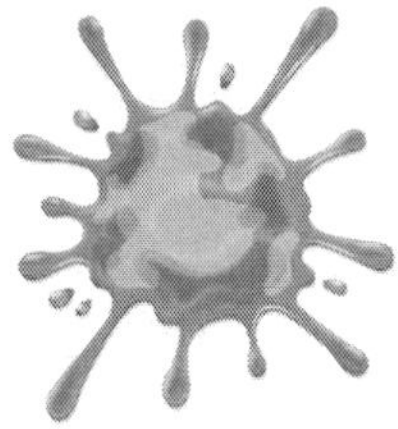

THE POEMS

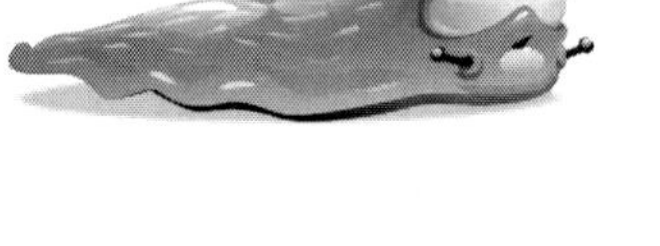

Lillo, The Messy Mosnter

As I sleep, I hear my naughty monster,
He feels very soft, like a fluffy cat,
He smells like rotten eggs,
He can scare me, but not much.

His red horns are like the scales on a fish,
One horn is small and stubby,
The other is skinny and pointy,
His little, red nose is shiny,
Sometimes, I think he is a clown.

He has big, stubby teeth,
But some can be small,
His feet sound like big thuds,
He nearly wakes up the house!

His name is Lillo, the messy monster,
Beware, sleep with one eye open!
He will make your room messy,
But, I still love him!

Maizie Fraser (10)
Alehousewells Primary School, Kemnay

The Homework Monster

The hungry homework monster
With its big, red, hairy head,
The hungry homework monster
Waits underneath your bed,
The sneaky homework monster,
His antenna emits a sense of dread.

The mysterious homework monster
Munching maths with glee,
He drinks your spelling
Instead of his tea,
The smelly homework monster
Will bite your teacher's bread,
Has to correct your spelling
Which gives him a sore head.

But, when the sun comes up
And you don't have your homework,
Just remember the homework monster
Has been well-fed.

Jake Dunbar (10)
Alehousewells Primary School, Kemnay

Wolfie The Monster

His hairy fur makes you think in a blink,
His blood-red spikes come in the night,
My monster's scary, like Aunt Mary,
He's as hungry as one-thousand sharks.

In the night, he's scared of light
But that doesn't matter, he'll get you in a bite,
If you see him, he'll turn you into dust
If he must.

In the morning, he's full of mischief,
He'll swing on your lights,
He'll break your valuables.

He is looking for a friend, so don't be shy,
Wolfie is just a big sap!

Jordan Gray (9)
Alehousewells Primary School, Kemnay

Puff, Cute But Deadly

Puff is a very cute monster,
He has a black, sharp tail,
A pink, long tongue and tiny pink wings,
He is green and fluffy, like candyfloss.

Puff likes to watch you,
But you wouldn't know,
He's as sneaky as a rat,
He's as light as a feather,
Be careful, he is as hungry as a lion,
But, be aware, he's very deadly!

When you're sleeping,
You'll hear him bubbling,
Under your bed,
He'll suck your brain and blood,
Puff does look cute,
But he is very, very deadly.

Calum Brown (9)
Alehousewells Primary School, Kemnay

My Friend, Arexi

There is a monster
Under my bed,
Her name is Arexi
And her eyes are blood-red,
She has long, wavy, midnight-black hair,
Her teeth are so sharp it would give you a scare,
She has two different mouths, one for each food,
Like carrots, potatoes and delicious steak stew!

Arexi is helpful in many different ways,
She could help you with your homework
Or put on a display
But, what she likes to do is very different,
Like running around meadows
And becoming breathless.

Mhairi Megan Kinghorn (10)
Alehousewells Primary School, Kemnay

The Midnight Snacker

I am Slimy Sid, but you can call me Sid,
I sneak around your house when you are asleep,
I raid your fridge at night,
There's nothing left for you to eat,
So, you rush to the shop and buy more for the night,
There is nothing left,
So my tummy rumbles like thunder,
So, when they come back, I was nice
And had one thing a night,
The kid named Sid said to me,
"You can sleep under my bed,
And I'll pass you something at night
Maybe my homework..."

Calum Wood (10)
Alehousewells Primary School, Kemnay

Monster All Over The City

My monster's name is Alex,
He is very spotty,
Has a long tongue, red eyes, horns,
A big mouth and a red body,
He is as hungry as a tiger,
His belly rumbles like rain,
He has big eyes.

His is like a tiger with stripes
And like a dinosaur with spikes,
He is a gentle monster and very fluffy,
He is as nice as a teddy bear.

He is sleepy and lazy,
Like a dog in his bed,
He is a cuddly little monster
And he is a good storyteller too!

Derren Wilson (10)

Alehousewells Primary School, Kemnay

The Hungry Beast

This hungry beast
Is hungrier than a thousand sharks,
He smells like old shoes,
When he speaks, he echoes loudly,
When I touch his hairy fur, it feels so tickly.

He is as spooky as a ghost,
He is as red as blood,
Beware, he will get you in your sleep!
He is as big as a dragon,
He sleeps with an open eye,
He can smell you from far away.

He thuds really loudly when he is ready for dinner,
Goodnight,
Gobble, gobble, gobble!

Lily Shewan (9)
Alehousewells Primary School, Kemnay

Vengence's Bite

When he sneaks after me
With jaws as wide as a bus,
He's going to eat me up!
I know it, so there's not much point in running.

He's as fast as two Formula One cars
Going at top speed,
I'm his prey,
He won't delay in gobbling me up,
His scaly skin is like a snake's,
Making him streamlined,
His teeth are pearly black, as sharp as a wolf's,
He's as big as two schools in length
And as wide as a car.

Jayden Shek (10)
Alehousewells Primary School, Kemnay

Zack The Monster

My monster is called Zack,
Zack has black fur, orange wings and massive fangs,
He lives in Monsterville, he is the best known monster there,
He is very silly and can take a joke.

Zack's favourite food is a crisp sandwich,
His favourite drink is Diet Coke,
He is obsessed with Coke.

He seems scary but he isn't at all,
He is sweet,
Zack would never hurt a fly,
That was a lie, he just ate one!
Run, flies, run!

Amy-Lea Gillies (9)
Alehousewells Primary School, Kemnay

The Bloogamo

His fur is as blue as the morning sky,
When he sings, it sounds like a soothing lullaby,
His eyes are orange and pink,
The pink is as bright as candyfloss,
His orange iris is as orange as a blazing fire.

His strawberry-red branch legs are super knobbly,
They crackle each time he moves his red legs,
His big, disgusting feet have warts made out of tree bark,
His big, sharp teeth won't hurt a fly,
But maybe his little teeth.

Keelin Whyte (10)
Alehousewells Primary School, Kemnay

Foxyness, The King Of Monsters

Foxyness is my monster,
He sleeps under my bed,
Foxyness is my friend,
We wear the same bands,
He smells like royalty
And looks like a unicorn.

His marmalade tail spins like a helicopter,
His ears are like a cat,
His black ear in the middle is like a unicorn,
His nose is like an upside-down heart,
He's forgetful as well.

Foxyness, my monster,
He is my best friend
With his little stick eyes.

Owen Stuart (10)
Alehousewells Primary School, Kemnay

Terry's Friend Hunt

The ever-so lonely Terry, in all his loneliness,
He just needs a friend,
He can never get a friend
No matter what,
People say he is scary,
People say he is mean.

People never liked him,
People always hit him,
They never liked his big eyes
Or his deep-black wings,
But, one day, he met another monster
Called the Fluffy Bloogamo.

All he ever wanted was a hug
From a really fluffy friend.

Ayden Jones (10)
Alehousewells Primary School, Kemnay

Fuzzy The Monster

This is Fuzzy, the monster,
She is really, really kind,
She won't hurt you
But she might if you're bad.

Fuzzy is fat but she is really cute,
She has fur all over her tummy,
Fuzzy has one big eye,
She is light blue and pink.

She's as slow as a sloth,
Her two legs are really slow,
Her body, it's as fluffy as a pom-pom,
She smells like lavender.

Sophie Louise Stephen (9)
Alehousewells Primary School, Kemnay

Cutie

My monster's name is Cutie,
She is fluffy like candyfloss,
She is blue like the sky,
She helps people,
She moves like a human.

She likes to eat blueberries,
Sometimes, she eats strawberries,
She hums beautiful music
And she has friends called Cat Bear and Glory!

Kirsty Alex McGhee (11)
Alehousewells Primary School, Kemnay

The Beautiful Disaster Who Was An Alien!

T here was a very rainy day, it was too miserable to go out!
H orrifyingly, there was a massive lightning flash.
E evee ran inside for the beautiful disaster was coming!

B en pushed Eevee into the closet and got his wolf claws.
"E llo!" a voice said. She was here - but Ben wasn't scared!
A fter a while, there was no noise, but red dripped.
U *s wolves will win!* Eevee thought. Little did she know
T hat the Beautiful Disaster was an alien in a robot suit!
I n a while, the front door slammed open!
"F BI, open up!" It was the FBI! They were going to take the alien away!
U ber drivers crowded around the house in awe!
L ittle did they know, the Beautiful Disaster escaped!

D isaster came back a few days later to tickle them.
I t was now sunny, so Ben and Eevee went out to play,
S o the Beautiful Disaster wanted to play, but it couldn't
A nd it disguised itself as a human and went to play!
S oon, when it was the end of the day, the Disaster couldn't go back to normal.
T errified, it went to find help, but it was the only monster on Earth!
"E ek!" she squealed when something tapped her.
"R oar!" the thing roared - it was another alien! It helped the Disaster, then it went to her own planet.

Evie Blackwell (11)

Cathkin Primary School, Cambuslang

The Opposite

T errifyingly, I sat up and saw
H airy legs at my door
E ruption came from the walls

O bviously, I screamed and
P anicked a lot
P ointy ears peeped round my door
"O h dear!" I said to myself
S ick came into my mouth, but
I got out from under my covers and
T he hairy legs and pointy ears were just another
E xcitement ball that I loved and cared about so much!

Marlie Martin (10)
Cathkin Primary School, Cambuslang

Withery

W hen night came
I t was time for Withery to become wicked
T he next day, it looked like nothing
H appened, but
E verybody knew, especially the parents whose child was missing
R evolting to them it was, they knew it was the monster
Y elping, the parents knew without a doubt...

Sami Uzuntok (11)
Cathkin Primary School, Cambuslang

The Monster That Lives Under My Bed

The monster that lives under my bed
is as pink as Santa's cheeks.
The monster that lives under my bed
has boots like squeaky mice.
The monster that lives under my bed
is as friendly as a dolphin.
The monster that lives under my bed
has teeth as white as pearls.
The monster that lives under my bed
is as bouncy as a trampoline.
The monster that lives under my bed
is as fluffy as a blanket.
The monster that lives under my bed
is as squishy as a marshmallow.
The monster that lives under my bed
is as big as a tractor.
The monster that lives under my bed
is made of candyfloss.

Clementine Gemmell (10)
Craigclowan Preparatory School, Perth

The Monster That Searches For Me

I could hear it stomping around, the monster that searches for me,
His legs are like big trees!

His pitch-black eyes like a dark, cold night,
The monster that searches for me.

The monster that searches for me,
He has sharp claws like knives.

The monster that searches for me,
Has teeth as sharp as swords.

The monster that searches for me,
His whole body is as tall as a skyscraper.

The monster that searches for me,
Has a mouth that is like an endless void.

The monster that searches for me in the night...

Aidan Slight (11)
Craigclowan Preparatory School, Perth

The Monster That Lives Under My Bed

The monster that lives under my bed
has eyes as blue as the sea.

The monster that lives under my bed
is as purple as beetroot.

The monster that lives under my bed
has boots as squeaky as a mouse.

The monster that lives under my bed
has teeth as sharp as thorns.

The monster that lives under my bed
has a tongue as rough as a cow's tongue.

The monster that lives under my bed
is as huge as a whale.

The monster that lives under my bed
has toenails as sharp as a chainsaw.

Melissa Stewart (11)
Craigclowan Preparatory School, Perth

My Spooky Monster

The monster that lives in my shed
has teeth like razor blades.

The monster that lives in my shed
is nasty like a shark.

The monster that lives in my shed
is as hungry as a whale.

The monster that lives in my shed
has hair as spiky as thorns.

The monster that lives in my shed
is as mischievous as a monkey.

The monster that lives in my shed
is as intriguing as a dragon.

The monster that lives in my shed
is lonely.

Andrew Gordon (11)
Craigclowan Preparatory School, Perth

I Am The Monster

I am the monster as fluffy as a cloud,
I am the monster as squishy as a marshmallow,
I am the monster as colourful as a rainbow,
I am the monster with a pyramid as small as an ant,
I am the monster as clean as shampoo,
I am the monster that was white as a sheep,
I am the monster as tall as you,
I am the monster as fast as a cheetah,
I am the monster as stealthy as a ninja,
I am the monster as harmless as a fish,
I am the monster as smart as a teacher.

Keir MacGregor (10)
Craigclowan Preparatory School, Perth

My Monster

The monster that lives under my trampoline
can run as fast as a fairy.
The monster that lives under my trampoline
snores as loud as the thunder.
The monster that lives under my trampoline
is as spooky as a ghost.
The monster that lives under my trampoline
crawls onto my trampoline and flips like an acrobat.
The monster that lives under my trampoline
is called Soloflow 8.
The monster that lives under my trampoline
is as kind as a puppy.

Leo Reid (10)
Craigclowan Preparatory School, Perth

Subject 12063

The monster who hunts living kind,
Who is as wide as a city,
Who is as round as a doughnut,
The monster is as big as the sun,
It's as tall as a skyscraper,
Tentacles as long as a whale,
Rusty teeth like a sunken ship,
Blows more flames than a dragon,
Fires artillery shells more powerful than a nuke,
Has nukes more dangerous than the Death Star,
As heavy as a planet,
Stirs like an earthquake.

Alex Morren (11)
Craigclowan Preparatory School, Perth

My Monster

The monster that lives under the stairs has claws like sharp knives,
The monster that lives under the stairs laughs like a clown,
The monster that lives under the stairs has eyes as red as blood,
The monster that lives under the stairs has horns like saws,
The monster that lives under the stairs is as green as slime,
The monster that lives under the stairs has teeth like diamonds.

Peter Magnus Wang (11)
Craigclowan Preparatory School, Perth

The Monster That Lives Under My Bed

The monster that lives under my bed
has horns as sharp as thorns.

The monster that lives under my bed
has teeth as yellow as mustard.

The monster that lives under my bed
has eyes as red as a burning flame.

The monster that lives under my bed
is as scary as a vampire.

The monster that lives under my bed
roars like thunder.

Hannah Mary McPherson (11)
Craigclowan Preparatory School, Perth

Under My Bed

The monster that lives under my bed has teeth as white as snow,
And is warm as a melted marshmallow,
My monster has eyes like blueberries,
And a body like an ice lolly,
My monster has horns as colourful as a rainbow,
And she is as kind as God,
Her arms smell like delicious cupcakes fresh from the oven.

Carla Cumming (10)

Craigclowan Preparatory School, Perth

My Monster Poem

The monster that lives in my closet is as huge as a bus,
The monster that lives in my closet has teeth like razor blades,
The monster that lives in my closet is strong like the Hulk,
The monster that lives in my closet is fierce like a tiger,
The monster that lives in my closet, his eyes are as red as a fire.

Sasha Pibworth (11)
Craigclowan Preparatory School, Perth

My Monster

My massive monster mumbled under my bed,
His tummy was rumbling underneath me,
I looked under my bed and saw the ugliest thing ever,
It had a green body, ergh! It gave me goosebumps,
It had horns like a devil,
Purple like plums.

Mark Anderson (10)

Craigclowan Preparatory School, Perth

My Scary Monster

M y monster is massive as a skyscraper
O ily, bloody arms
N oisy as a rock band
S cary as a black panther
T eeth as massive as knives
E vil as hornets
R eckless as Voldemort.

Tom MacWilliam (10)
Craigclowan Preparatory School, Perth

The Friendly Monster Poem

There is a friendly monster named Horny Borny
He likes to give his brother and sister a huge fright by jumping on their backs
Horny Borny always falls over and stubs his paw and it is painful
He likes to roar so loud that your ears go pop!
Horny Borny is so fluffy that you can use him as a pillow
He smells some delicious food
He smalls bacon so tasty
Horny Borny slavers worse than a dog
Horny Borny is as tall as the Eiffel Tower
His ears are as big as a trumpet
He launched a firework and it went *bang!*
He loves to jump in puddles, so he went outside when it was raining
He jumped in one and it made a massive splash!

Aiden Matthew Nicholson (8)
Fair Isle Primary School, Kirkcaldy

The Night Flyer In The Night

In the night, don't make a peep
There is a monster who likes to creep
It is evil, giant and it can even fly
It is like a roaring lion without food to say bye to
Kids are its favourite food to be eaten
Its name is Ghosty the rustling monster
It can take flight, even with a lobster
He whooshes to homes for dinner
He's thinner than everyone, way thinner
Remember, don't look, don't cry, don't make a peep
Or it will eat and make you creep
It makes a huge bang for a little snore
It can always eat more
Do you believe me?
Make a peep at night and see
It is the end of the night for you and me!

Ben James William Inglis (8)
Fair Isle Primary School, Kirkcaldy

The Day Cuty Pie Got Adopted

One stormy night, a monster was out, rustling through the leaves
You wouldn't believe an adorable monster could be so lonely
Cuty Pie's the name
And love's her game
She is as cute as a cat
She is as friendly as a puppy
She got trapped in a cage
And put in a cot
Cuty Pie flew like a bat
And got back to the wild
But the child ran after
Cuty Pie got faster and got away
But she got caught and taken home
On the way
They saw a gnome
Cuty Pie got put into the bath
Her hair started to fizz like a bath bomb!

Kalleigh Lockhart (8)
Fair Isle Primary School, Kirkcaldy

The Rainbow Monster

In the morning, he comes out to play
His name is Wubbles
He just wants lovely cuddles
If you hug him, he will eat you up
In one big gulp
If you go up close
You'll faint right under his nose
He's hungry as a lion
He runs like a dinosaur
Better worry, he's a carnivore
When he goes under clouds
It starts to rain
It gives the clouds massive pain
If you go to his house
He will lock you up
He will put you in a cup
But he will be a clown, he might bite
He will always give you a giant fright!

Aiden Robertson (8)
Fair Isle Primary School, Kirkcaldy

The Giant Spider

Colossal Spider has a thousand legs
He is blacker than the blackest of black
He grew too many legs
He spins webs like a propeller
He has eyes as red as blood
He is pure evil.

Lukas Kerr (8)
Fair Isle Primary School, Kirkcaldy

Inside Your Mind

S omething in your mind scratching loudly
C reeping around feeding on your ear wax
R attling your mind, is it a nightmare?
A loud echo you can hear driving you insane
T easing your mind
C heat once, cheat twice, but with Scratch no cheats allowed
H ere's a hint, she's very playful

I magine if it was real, what would you feel
S ee her once, see her twice... Now that's rare

H ere you go, you see her, isn't she ugly?
E ar wax everywhere but does it feel better?
R eally? You thought it was real?
E veryone hates her but do you?

Hailey Black (10)
High Mill Primary School, Carluke

The Happy Monster

My little monster is bright green
He is very smart but certainly not mean
If you see him in the street he will say hi
But in a couple of minutes, he might say bye
If he meets a boy or girl he will jump up
This little monster went to school
And by the time he was eight, he could play pool
He goes to bed at 7:30
But one night he fell out of bed and got very hurty
The fast ambulance went as fast as could be
And he got to hospital at 7:33
He ended up with a broken arm
It was definitely not a false alarm.

Zoe Thomson (8)
High Mill Primary School, Carluke

It's Here, Run!

S harpening her cleavers every night
H orns like a rhino ready to strike
E yes, she's got three, it's freaky you see
S eek her in the forest, beware, she'll see you.

C laws for hands, one hit and you're out cold
O nly seen in the dead of night
M urder scenes have been found where she kills
I f she is frightened she will teleport
N ewspapers have been filled with her news
G entle is a stranger to her.

Cayden Williamson (8)
High Mill Primary School, Carluke

Gruffs Scruffs

G rizzly gruff's up ahead
R un far, far away!
U p up high on a hill
F un you have up there
F orever friends are the gruffs
S unny times they have so much

S tash of food they have to eat
C ats are their favourite pets
R unning is their favourite sport
U p to the top of a hill
F un
F un with the scruffs
S unny times they have so much.

Yvie Kerr (9)
High Mill Primary School, Carluke

Blobby

M y Blobby is scary but really kind
Y ellow is the big spotty colour.

M r Blobby is a blob but has sharp teeth
O nly I am not scared of Blobby
N o one should hate monsters because they're nice
S o scary, no he's not
T oo bad he is short but I love you Blobby
E ven if you're really bad
R eally no one likes you, it's only me.

Brooke Black (8)
High Mill Primary School, Carluke

Fluffyblossom

I can feel fluffy things.
I can hear a band in my room.
I can taste a little fluffy hair.
I can smell a little dog's breath.
I can see weird fluffy things.

I can feel water in my bed.
I can hear banging in the bathroom.
I can taste yummy Coco Pops in my mouth.
I can smell monster slime.
I can see monster hair all over my bed.

Leland George Flynn (11)
High Mill Primary School, Carluke

The Spooky Fang Man

It was one dark night
Every child was asleep
But one boy couldn't sleep
A stink of a smell
And Fang Man returned
He had sharp nails and said,
"Time to kill!"
If you go to the woods
You are in for a scare
As he is out there still
To kill.

Cohen Dobbin (8)
High Mill Primary School, Carluke

Very Fluffy

I can smell slime when you're under my bed
I can hear scary noises on my bed
I can hear little green monsters in the street
I can hear little noisy monsters in the car
I can hear a little monster in bed
I can hear a little scared monster too.

Lexi Black (7)
High Mill Primary School, Carluke

The Never

As black as night
Monsters are slimy
Monsters are dark
Monsters are flying
Monsters are powerful
Monsters are scary
Monsters are made out of lava
Monsters are evil.

Ela Nur Isik (6)
High Mill Primary School, Carluke

Jelly, The Scary Monster

I can hear growls in my cupboard
I can smell its smelly breath
I can feel its blue fur with my hand
I can taste its breath
I check in my cupboard
But there is nothing there.

Zak Skelton (8)
High Mill Primary School, Carluke

The Monster Under My Bed

During the day, he roams quietly under my bed,
but...
At night, he emerges from his hiding place,
Like a snake ambushing its prey.
The monster introduces himself as Mouthy,
With a humongous mouth filled with 5,000 teeth,
Square eyes and no nose,
Mouthy looks like an abomination!
He has black fur like a grizzly bear and is as tall as
a skyscraper!
When he talks, his tongue flaps around,
Making a loud, slurping sound.
Apart from this, the room is silent.
All of a sudden, *boom!*
The closet door is forced open,
And another monster appears with a loud *thud!*
He is spotty like a cheetah,
But thankfully, less scary-looking than Mouthy!
Walking quietly towards the door,
I attempt to make an escape.

"Where are you going?" ask the two monsters
aggressively.
I don't reply...
Just keep on going!

Callan Mackay (9)

Melvich Primary School, Melvich

A Monster Lurking Down The Stairs

Having a sleepover at Grandma's house,
The place is as quiet as a mouse.
Suddenly, I hear something downstairs!
"Grandma, is that you down there?"
She doesn't respond, which is rare.
On the stairs, I see orange hairs,
Reminding me of a past nightmare.
I hear a voice from the bathroom,
Feeling scared, I grab a broom!
Carefully approaching the room that calls my name,
I'm relieved that everything looks the same!
Suddenly, a rainbow splash blasts out of the sink,
Saying, "Hello, my name is Link!"
Staring at a brightly-coloured monster with a million eyes and feet,
Grandma suddenly bursts into the room, much to my relief!

Sam Heddle (10)
Melvich Primary School, Melvich

Monsters Meeting

Hearing the birds chirp in the morning wakes me with a smile.
I love the cool breeze blowing gently against my fuzzy fur.
Today, I am meeting my two friends, Spellbound and Fangs.
Spellbound is as bright as a light covered by yellow fluff,
Fangs is as fit as an athlete and as bendy as a gymnast.
We join together for lunch,
It's sushi for me, curry for Spellbound and super spicy salad for Fangs.
Watching a marvellous monster movie is next.
After a time, sleep overcomes me and I slither to bed like a snake, but...
My monster friends have endless energy!
Spellbound heads for yoga whilst Fangs makes her way to the gym.
I just want to sleep for a year!

Eevie Mackay (9)

Melvich Primary School, Melvich

Carl And The Cyborg Cake Cruncher

Carl is as tall as the extreme depth of Loch Ness
and as chubby as four hundred rhinos put
together,
His metal feet stomp through London,
They go *bang, boom, crash* and *clink!*
Tripping over Tower Bridge.
The nasty stench of his unwashed body travels to
the other side of the world.
He has four dull eyes, a pig-like nose and three
giant mouths filled with teeth as sharp as razors.
His head is as bald as a chocolate bar and his ears
look like two droning chanters.
The cyborg is a greedy pig, always desperate to
devour delicious cake.

Donald Farquhar (11)
Melvich Primary School, Melvich

The Spiky Sea Anemone

Crumble, a tiny sea creature, is as cunning as a fox,
A black and spiky anemone with stick-like feet,
It will viciously sting you with its sharp, scissor-like spikes if you're not careful,
When in the greeny-blue sea.
Never alone, Crumble is always surrounded by fellow sea anemones,
Intending to cause havoc.
The naughty anemone has a very different appearance from his friends,
With squinting eyes and grey lips.
In the dark depths of the sea,
He waits for unsuspecting victims who seek to enter his territory.

Josefine Holroyd (10)
Melvich Primary School, Melvich

The Dark Appearance

M arionette is as black as tar
A lways waiting to pounce on innocent sleeping children
R eeking of terrible toilets and stinking sewers
I nk covers her entire body
O n her hands are sharp claws ready to attack
N eon cheeks, lips and tears characterise her face
E ager for a scare, she will not fail
T hree oddly-shaped eyes with a piercing look
T he Marionette is as tall as a giraffe
E verywhere you look, she will be there.

Dylan Mackay (10)
Melvich Primary School, Melvich

Dots The Cyclops

Dots loves ladybirds, particularly his precious pet called Spot.
As an animal lover, he is a vegetarian.
Dots lives in a cosy cave deep in the forest.
Colourful, spotty with a rainbow belly and as tall as a tower,
He has pointed horns and antennae which do not match.
Dots is as silly as a monkey and as bonkers as a brush,
Jumping around like a gymnast, he enjoys nature and being outdoors.
A unique and friendly monster,
Always eager to play!

Zara Mackintosh (9)
Melvich Primary School, Melvich

Mr Smell Socks

Smell Socks
He is stinky, but not so dinky
Smell Socks
He rocks in his favourite socks
Smell Socks
Has an eye for a very large pie
But so does his friend Brian the fly

Smell Socks and Brian the fly
Begin to eat the pie
But Smell Socks forgets all about Brian
And eats the fly with the pie!

Benny Mackinnon (8)
Melvich Primary School, Melvich

The Mysterious Mr Moohead

As I sneak around the village of Melvich,
I smell the minging, monstrous children.
My boss, Mr Crabhead, is as crabby as a crab,
Telling me to terrorise children whilst they sleep.
He plans to have a fantastic feast of horrid children!
I capture them from their dreams,
Scaring them to death!

Marielle Mackay (9)
Melvich Primary School, Melvich

The Weight Lifter

Weight Lifter is as spiky as a hedgehog
He is strong like The Rock
He has red horns like a devil
He is blue like a blueberry
He lifts heavy weights 'cause he's a weightlifter
He eats cats and dogs
Spiky, that's how he is, so spiky
He rides UFOs straight out of Area 51
'Cause he's a member
He is the protector of the aliens
He is scary, that's how he scares off all the people that try to trespass
The scary dark gate like a hungry lion.

Viktor Tarev (9)
Our Lady Of Loretto Primary School, Dalmuir

All About Ziggy Zaggy

Here comes Ziggy Zaggy, walking down the halls
Then he goes back and comes with his football.
After that, he goes to bed
And then, in the morning, he turns red.
When he is red, he goes to bed
When he wakes up, he becomes dead.
When he is dead, he goes to the zoo
Then after that, he goes to the loo.
Ziggy Zaggy's teeth are as long and sharp as the corner of a ping pong table.
His body is as spiky as a crocodile
So you never want to see him in your life!

Leila Hopkins (9)
Our Lady Of Loretto Primary School, Dalmuir

The Night Monster

Spocks lurks in pitch-blackness when no one is watching.
He sneaks in the trash, waiting for food!
When someone sees him, he disappears in darkness!
If you saw Spocks, you would get a deadly feeling near him,
Also, if you even try to kill him, remember,
He hears everything!
Remember that, if you hear the sound like this,
Creak!
Run for your life if you want to live!

Migle Zaleckyte (9)
Our Lady Of Loretto Primary School, Dalmuir

The Lazy Old Monster

My monster's eyes are as red as rubies
Glistening in the sun.
His eyes are like burning coal.
My monster has blood dripping,
Dripping from his spikes.
His spikes are as sharp as teeth.
My monster's body smell is very vile!
He smells like garbage that is 100 days old,
He smells like cheese that is out of date!
My monster is stinky as a rotten egg.

Hamad Shahid (9)

Our Lady Of Loretto Primary School, Dalmuir

Pinkeinke

Hello, my name is Pinkeinke
and I am scary as a grizzly bear!
I love eating children
and they're very tasty to eat
especially if they are asleep!
I love it!
They are delicious
and for my drink with lovely children
I have a nice drink of blood!
My favourite food is a raw flesh soup for lunch
and for breakfast, it's raw chicken!

Robyn Gourlay (8)
Our Lady Of Loretto Primary School, Dalmuir

Colourful Zingy

Zingy's hair is long as a cable.
His teeth are sharp as a crocodile's.
He is spiky as a tree branch.
He is scary as a devil.
He is silly as a sloth.
He is colourful as a rainbow.
He is terrifying as a clown.
If you ever see him, run away
Because he is so many things!
He could do anything to you
So watch out for him!

Isla Yvonne McHugh (9)
Our Lady Of Loretto Primary School, Dalmuir

Sharpelier

This monster is on the loose
Every winter while you are in your homes
It is looking for a place of its own
It has the sharpest blades in town
Sounds friendly and nice
But it likes to eat children, it can't deny
It hides in the snowy night!
Beware, or you might get a fright
Its name is Sharpelier
Wow, what a night!

Mwitwa Sitembo (8)
Our Lady Of Loretto Primary School, Dalmuir

Sanna The Sweet Monster

The girl Sanna was very sweet and kind for a monster,
She was the sweetest monster in town!
She had curly hair like a bear,
She had lava in her veins like the rain.

She was the biggest monster in town,
Sanna slept through the raindrops, *drip, drip, drip.*
Everyone was scared of her,
But she enjoyed how she was.

Ellie McCluskie (8)
Our Lady Of Loretto Primary School, Dalmuir

My Monster

My monster is a shape-shifter
It might be your friend,
It might be you
His name is Spikey Dave
The stuff he drinks is blood
He's always bloodthirsty or a vampire
He lives in a house as old as can be
Where people lived but not anymore as they are dead
He is as fast as a cheetah
And as quiet as a mouse.

Austin Charles Currie (9)
Our Lady Of Loretto Primary School, Dalmuir

Mega Morph

His teeth are as sharp as blades
and if you don't like him
he will fade.
He is very scary
and very hairy.
He is not very spotty
but he is very naughty.
Only sometimes, he is gentle.
He is giant
so never annoy him!

Nathan Mbambi (9)
Our Lady Of Loretto Primary School, Dalmuir

Einstein's Life

Einstein the Frankenstein, ugly as can be,
His favourite thing to eat is toenails for tea.
He lives in a cave, small and hollow,
He will gobble you up with one swallow.
Now you know what he is like,
Good luck sleeping tonight!

Fynlay Foreman (9)
Our Lady Of Loretto Primary School, Dalmuir

Strawberry Patches

Hi, my name is Strawberry Patches
I am as cute as a bunny
Soft as a pillow.
I have whiskers like a cat
Meow!
For a snack, I like to eat children
And I have one brother
And an ugly sister called Anguglya!

Anna Devlin (9)
Our Lady Of Loretto Primary School, Dalmuir

Mr Hairy

He is a monster
As you see him
You will pee!
You need to run
So you don't get caught
If you are lucky
He will not eat you
You should run just to be safe
His mouth is not the best.

Jayden Owens (9)
Our Lady Of Loretto Primary School, Dalmuir

Jef

J agged arms and legs,
E vil brothers make fun of him,
F antastic colours

T he eyes he has can see through wood,
H e smells like sweets,
E asily distinguishable

H appily walks down the street,
A pples are his favourite food,
P reviously naughty
P lus, he devours cake,
Y ounger than most monsters

M achine heart is gas-powered,
O ften refuses to move from his home,
N ot as tall as other monsters,
S till loves his house,
T astes like a vampire,
E nthusiastic about what he hears,
R ock-hard arms contain happiness.

Daniel Roulston (8)
Ratho Primary School, Ratho

Charlie The Monster

C harlie is always up to mischief,
H e will eat anything,
A smell of stinky, rotten eggs,
R oar as loud as a T-rex,
L ong, big fangs,
I ncredibly big body,
E normous wings as rigid as a sword,

T ongue as long as a lizard's,
H e sometimes hides under my bed,
E normously big claws,

M onstrous behaviour,
O ld as the world,
N aughty as a cheeky monkey,
S trong as a gorilla,
T errifyingly enormous, spiky tail,
E normously big wings,
R obotic heart so he lives forever.

Cameron Mowat (8)
Ratho Primary School, Ratho

Devil Dan

Devil Dan is smelly like a rotten egg,
He sounds like an evil man,
He looks like a big ball of hair,
Devil Dan tastes like human hearts,
He feels like a beast with the hair all over,
He creeps around the woods at night,
Will you be his next victim?
Do you think so?
Oh, you said no?
I guess we'll find out soon!
Don't you dare go into the woods alone,
He's got red eyes,
He's dark and hairy,
Also, he is a shape-shifter,
He's just around the corner
And, if you're not careful,
He will eat you!

Penny Prudence Watson (8)
Ratho Primary School, Ratho

Abominable Almighty

His eyes are like red, fiery bombs
His breath smells like burning tyres
He is fierce like the wind in winter
The touch of him is hairy and feels like fangs and mould
He is a bag of evil
He talks dreadfully like an aggressive lion
He has snake arms that poison you
Go ahead, if you dare
If you dare to get brainwashed
Mua ha ha!
I'm waiting, I'm not harmful,
Come on, that's it...
Kill! Die! Kill! Kill! Die!
Well, that went well, didn't it?

Alysha Dosanjh (8)
Ratho Primary School, Ratho

Maddie The Make-Up Monster

My name is Maddie,
I never give up,
I love to do make-up
And I have my own shop
Where monsters can get things
And have their make-up done,
Why am I not scary, you might ask?
Well, because some monsters are not scary,
I am extremely kind and helpful
But I love to play with my friends,
My best friend is Grace,
We love to play together,
I have a lot of other friends,
I love to be kind,
It leaves a warm feeling in my tummy,
If you are kind
You will feel the same way!

Gracie Mackie (8)
Ratho Primary School, Ratho

Fuzzy

My monster smells
Like a giant pile of muddy washing and smelly slime,
It feels like a blob of wobbly jelly,
It feels like a dark rainbow
From the outer space galaxy,
It sounds like a big, ferocious tiger,
It likes to eat garlic,
She lives in Monster Land,
She loves to play with her friends,
She loves where she lives,
Her favourite colour is green,
She likes to be kind and caring,
She thinks you should be kind to others too,
I love monsters and I think you should too!

Jessica Lynes (8)
Ratho Primary School, Ratho

Painful Paralysing Poppy

Welcome, only enter if you want to risk your life
Many people don't enter
Only five people have entered and died
Poppy is very dangerous
Her eyes are yellow, blinding, disturbing, terrifying
Her breath smells of fire, smoke, sewer water
She is as fast as a flash of lightning
Her touch feels like spikes, thorns, needles all together
She is terrifying, spooky and nervewracking
She is very violent to new people, even monsters
But she is not as soon as you get to know her.

Freya Alice Stevenson (8)
Ratho Primary School, Ratho

Skrack

He's as savage as a T-rex,
He has scaly skin,
He has extremely deadly tentacles,
He smells like slime,
He's the king of ferocious birds,
He has five, fierce orange eyes,
He hisses through the sky,
He has three ferocious fangs,
He's a six-winged fury,
His skin is black,
Eyes on antenna,
He lives in a cave.
So stay under your covers!
You might be eaten whole!
He might be getting ready,
For his next supper,
It might be you!

Cameron McLaren (8)
Ratho Primary School, Ratho

Cotton Candy

"Hi, my name is Cotton Candy,
I am a monster,
I am very cute, pretty, fluffy, gentle and ferocious,
Not your normal monster!"
Cotton Candy looks yummy,
Cotton Candy, what else does she look like?
She likes art,
Her new bow is really pretty,
She will never leave it!
Her hair blows in the wind,
It is just beautiful,
I love her dress,
It reminds me of putty,
She loves unicorns and mermaids and fairies!

Isla McKinnon (8)
Ratho Primary School, Ratho

Mr Fireball

Fireball's eyes are dark, shiny and gold
His breath smells like flames on fire
He moves as quick as lightning
He feels all spiky and thorny
He's holding a bloody head
A tentacle will get you in a flash
He's carrying a bag of lightning
Around him there is always lightning striking
He has a furry bat around him
Near him, you will never see the light of day again.

Alex McIntosh (8)
Ratho Primary School, Ratho

The Chop Monster

My monster has super-tangled arms,
He has got special, rapid feet,
His big arm has big chains,
He can chop,
He has a humongous twelve-pack,
And he has been prohibited from lots of things,
He has got humongous teeth,
He smells like rotten eggs,
And he feels like solid rock,
He has really red eyes,
He looks like a walking devil,
And he's a Minotaur.

Noah Barrie (8)
Ratho Primary School, Ratho

Monster Cool

My monster bites all the time,
My monster is as scary as a T-rex,
My monster is so greedy,
People get really horrified by my monster,
My monster has one arm spike,
Monsters are so smelly, like rotten eggs,
My monster has spiky legs,
My monster is so evil,
My monster has three eyes,
My monster has red skin,
My monster is happy,
My monster is annoying.

James Littlejohn (7)
Ratho Primary School, Ratho

The Clown Gang

Their eyes droop like blood
They lurk in the sewers
They rot every day
They feel like mouldy goo
They smell of out-of-date milk
They carry knives of stress
If you touch them, you will be a psycho
You will regret living if you go near
Beware, watch your step
You will have a nightmare
Come play with us in the sewers
Ha ha ha!

Natalie Kirsty Wiszniewski (8)
Ratho Primary School, Ratho

Fluffy Pie

F luffy is very cute,
L ovely and pink, candyfloss is her favourite,
U nder the surface of the invisible planet she lives,
F riendly and amazingly kind,
F luffy loves abstract art,
Y ou would love to meet her.

P retty pink,
I absolutely love her,
E very day, she always smiles.

Maisie McCulloch (7)
Ratho Primary School, Ratho

Monster Horror

Up high in the mountains,
A monster they say,
He lives in the cave,
He smells like a pile of mud,
He has tentacles instead of legs,
Do you dare to enter?
And, he can't stand light,
He has wings like a dragon,
Horns like a bull,
He has a long, black tongue,
My monster has sharp claws,
He has four, huge arms
And he loves to frighten people.

Danny Curry (7)
Ratho Primary School, Ratho

Bob The Monster

Bob the monster,
He is very loud,
He is extremely slimy,
He is extremely greedy,
He is big but he can turn very small,
He is bigger than Earth,
He is extremely smelly,
He does not know maths,
He is as ugly as a witch,
My monster is as hungry as a T-rex,
My monster is extremely angry,
He is very ruthless,
He has ten heads.

Lachlan Morgan (8)
Ratho Primary School, Ratho

Bloby Junior

B eware, Bloby's about,
L onely as a ghost,
O nly I can help him,
B lack-tongued bandit,
Y awning every night,

J umping monster,
U nadventurous,
N o one would dare eat him,
I nside him, there is jelly,
O dd as a pancake,
R eading every day.

Freddie Hancock (8)
Ratho Primary School, Ratho

Boby

He smells like rotten eggs,
He looks like a pom-pom,
He likes shapes and sizes,
He plays on the swings with me and my brothers,
My monster has four eyes,
He keeps Sonic away,
I always talk to my monster,
My monster is ferocious
And I love him,
He is my BFF,
I will never forget him,
He will be in my heart forever.

Phoebe Dunlop (7)
Ratho Primary School, Ratho

Speedy Boy

Speed means a lot to Speedy Boy
Because he normally runs around,
To get fit, Speedy Boy can lift anything
With his invisible hands
And arms so epic that Speedy Boy
Could do one-hundred backflips in the air,
Speedy Boy is extremely fast,
So fast that he can deliver you anything you can imagine,
Speedy Boy's favourite food is diamond!

Kenzo Amankwah (8)
Ratho Primary School, Ratho

Zap!

A creepy lad
Travelling through electric cables
You can't hide from Zap
Eyes as white as snow
Smells like old blood
The reason he turned evil
Was he was a little boy with no friends
So one day he had had enough
This is his life now
He wants revenge
And he is going to do it with a bang!

Alasdair Forrest (8)
Ratho Primary School, Ratho

The Land Of Death

Once upon a time, there was an island
That had the most alarming creatures in the world
It is called The Land of Death
There is an electric ghost
Every time someone enters his lair, he is mad
The ghost is fierce but one person could beat him
So he did beat him up
And he was gone forever.

Cameron Mitchell (8)
Ratho Primary School, Ratho

Cute But Scary Monster

Warning, do not touch this monster
You could die
Big bold eyes as shiny as steel
Breath smells like rotten candy
Waddles around like a penguin
Feels super soft like the silkiest blanket
Whispers, "Touch me!"
Do not touch this monster,
Like I told you at the start.

Karis Adams (8)
Ratho Primary School, Ratho

Jellybean

Gigantic Jellybean is a monster,
Erupting jellybeans from his top hat,
Loud voice waking you up at night,
Large body shaped like a jellybean,
You wouldn't want to meet him or eat him,
Beastly!
Eats guacamole,
Atrociously bad,
Naughty and adorable.

Sam Crow (8)
Ratho Primary School, Ratho

Jianty

He was mighty but he was hunting for fish,
He was as slimy as dog food,
He is dark and he is waiting under your bed,
Waiting for you,
He gobbled everything up on Friday night,
My monster has two eyes,
My monster has a cheeky face,
My monster is big,
My monster has legs.

Arran Stevenson (8)
Ratho Primary School, Ratho

Fluffy The Monster

My monster smells of rotten eggs,
He tastes of a mouldy sandwich,
He sounds like a bus,
He looks like a cat,
He feels like a dog,
He is as strong as a lion,
His paws are as sticky as slime,
It has babies called Flufflings,
He loves Subway, Burger King and Dominos.

Noah Ssentamu (8)
Ratho Primary School, Ratho

Fiery Fiona

She likes the sun
But she loves the dark
She's just a child
But she's also a bat
She's got eyes as blue as the sea
She's as fast as a cheetah
Her touch feels as smooth as silk
She holds her knife to scare you away.

Kara Cowe (8)
Ratho Primary School, Ratho

Bad Boom

My monster is like rotten fish,
He sounds like a noisy classroom,
He feels like slime,
He has good moves and eyesight in the dark,
He smells like a rotten fish,
He is as tall as a skyscraper,
He jumps on people,
My monster is deadly.

Euan Ellis (7)
Ratho Primary School, Ratho

Concert Monster

The concert monster lives in Tuzunagi
He knows how to control minds
He has servants
His eyes are as red as blood
He smells like a dusty shelf
He's going as fast as light speed.

Aaron Biancalana (8)
Ratho Primary School, Ratho

Fluffball

Ellie reached under her bed to get her diary,
But instead, she felt something fluffy
So she went to pick it up
But it jumped out of her hand
She was so shocked,
She ran out of her room
When she came back in,
There was something in the middle of her room...
A little monster?
Then the monster said,
"Hi, my name is Fluff Ball,
And I am a friendly monster!"

Ellis McTeir (9)
Thorn Primary School, Johnstone

Fuzz Ball

This is Fuzz Ball
He is nice
He also holds a dice
He goes to people's houses
And cuddles them when they're sleeping
When he goes home, he starts leaping
He goes to school
He brings his bear to school
He pulls his bear into school
He is shy
But oh my
He's so friendly, but why?

Nicole Young (8)
Thorn Primary School, Johnstone

Scar

He is mean, he is small,
And you don't want to think about him at all
He may look harmless,
But he is charmless
Unless he steals you in the middle of the night
And gives you a fright
Then he'll keep you and squeeze you
Until you go back to sleep
Without a peep.

Corey David Geddes (9)
Thorn Primary School, Johnstone

Fatal Fernand

He's as hungry as a starving shark,
He's as fatal as a venomous snake,
He transforms a dream into a nightmare!
He sneaks in lots of houses
He eats tons of mice
He hides inside boxes
Waits for the perfect timing
To shout a horrid, "Boo!"

Emmanuel Okungbowa (9)
Thorn Primary School, Johnstone

One-Eyed Monster

As scary as a werewolf
And it's as funny as a clown
Its jaws are dog paws
And its teeth are like shark teeth
He's as hairy as a furball
And is as angry as a lion
He likes to fight and doesn't really win
He eats snails, but fails.

Jake Rutherford
Thorn Primary School, Johnstone

The Lurking Shadow

The goo in your room,
The one eye looking through your door,
The pink and yellow fluff in your mum's make-up,
At 3am, a shadow on your floor,
If you see these things in your house...
Beware! Boogey is on the loose!

Holly Hamilton (9)
Thorn Primary School, Johnstone

Zog

A one-eyed monster peeping through your door at night
Stay in your covers, nice and tight
Don't get a fright, he does not bite
Come out of your covers and say hello
He will be your friend all night long.

Carla Young (9)
Thorn Primary School, Johnstone

Spiky Wing

He is big and sad
Because he is so bad
Because his name is Spiky Wing
He sneaks in windows
And he creeps in a room
Sees a child
Then he is hiding in the corner
Waiting to attack...

Calum Johnston (9)
Thorn Primary School, Johnstone

Monster

He is spiky, he is strong
He isn't very long
Spikey is his name
And he isn't very tame!
He lurks down the street
And likes to eat meat.

Ryan Sprott (9)
Thorn Primary School, Johnstone

Good Monster Town

In Good Monster Town
It was peaceful until
Flame came into town and took over
He took people and made them slaves
Who can stop Flame?

Jamie Heron (8)
Thorn Primary School, Johnstone

A Monster But Not Like You

Walking in the park
And in the dark was a scaly monster,
Roaring as loud as a lion,
His eyes as dark as the night sky
And his mouth as wide as a mountain.

He is as bright as the light from the sun,
His teeth are as sharp as nails and very pale,
He really is a monster, but not like you.

He's friendly but hated,
But surely is the greatest,
He tends to be nice,
He trends like the friends,
But he really is a monster, but not like you.

He's a slug, he's very slow,
His hatred is now very low,
He really is a monster, but not like you.

Sophie Taylor (10)

Townhill Primary School, Townhill

My Monster

My monster has as many eyes
As there are stars in the sky,
Teeth as sharp as knives,
Oh, my!

Fur as soft as a baby's bum,
Legs as stubby as, oh no! Here he comes!
With his stubby legs, he wanders around in a great blunder
And his roar is as loud as thunder!

But, he has a heart and he can love
And he loves me, more than pancakes from my mum
And he watches over me as I sleep
And he doesn't get bored when I don't make a peep.

He comes with me to school,
And he's very fluffy, he's made of wool!
He watches over me, day and night
And when I wake him up, he doesn't put up a fight,
My monster is the best in the world

And his name is Eddy
And my monster is a teddy!

Ciara McNiece (10)
Townhill Primary School, Townhill

Never Sleep Again

Every night, the lava bat elemental monster
Comes out from the lava
And roams the city.

His eyes are as red as a demon,
If children are out at night,
In the morning, they are gone!

April to May, June to July,
September to October,
His skin is as wrinkly as a lizard.

No one wants to go out at night or sleep,
Do you want to go out?
No, no, no...
Do you want to die?

Consequently, he has no food,
So he is now dead,
The people are now safe again,
So sleep or go out at night,
But, be careful, he might still be out there!

Adam Hall (11)
Townhill Primary School, Townhill

My Monster

His eyes were yellow,
They were yellow as can be,
Seeing him riding on his scooter,
Deary me!

It was not just one eye,
Oh no, it was seven eyes!

His teeth were not the whitest of teeth,
Oh, and his teeth were daggers,
They're that sharp, it's true.

His spikes were the worst,
They were as sharp as a hedgehog,
Trust me.

His slimy trail is the colour of mossy-green,
You will never want to meet him.

He is a slug, but he is a cheetah,
He is so fast, oh, believe me!

Georgie Heddle (10)
Townhill Primary School, Townhill

Roary The Raging Monster

Roary the raging monster
Was the biggest, he was massive!
One day, he went to get
His teeth sharpened like daggers,
Plus, he was a slug,
Slow and ugly,
If only he was as beautiful as a pug!
And, his fur was as furry as can be!
His eyes were like crystals,
Shining big, but only when it was night,
He was also great at football,
He sent the defenders to the shop
To get an orange Fanta,
Topping it off with a beautiful banana!

Nathan Weir (10)
Townhill Primary School, Townhill

The Drool

His feet were as big as an elephant,
His jaw as wide as a house,
His nose swayed in the cool breeze,
His name is Oogley,
Only because he drools so much,
His drool is a slug,
It slowly drops down his face,
You never want to see him
Or he'll drool all over you.

His skin is as scaly as a snake,
You'd not want to touch it,
Also, it is covered in drool!
Oogley is still quite friendly,
But you'll get covered in drool!

Sophie Quoiani (10)
Townhill Primary School, Townhill

A Night Sky With A Light

As bright as the light yet
As dark as the night,
You have no idea how
She'll give you a fright!

She is a fright
But she is a light,
She doesn't bite,
Stay, it'll be alright.

It's just the torture
And the fright
That you'll go through
Tonight.

When she walks down the street,
Her heels click to the same, old beat,
But, you have no idea about the secrets
Lying at your feet.

Suriaya Khan (10)
Townhill Primary School, Townhill

The Alien Monster

This is Alien Monster,
It's got orange eyes
That are orange as burning fire,
It rhymes with amber orange.

He's a green and slimy monster
Because monsters are a bit slimy,
Rhymes with lime green.

He's got a big, slimy mouth,
It rhymes with flowers.

He's got long ears
And his ears are rhymed with long grass.

He's got big arms
And they are as thick as ribs.

Tiegan Ruby Shand (10)
Townhill Primary School, Townhill

The Spooky, Scary Creature

A monster named SSS slithers through the night,
His eyes are like pools of black ink
With red pupils that can shoot out lasers that are pink!
His teeth are as sharp as knives
And as white as snow,
His skin is as slimy as goo
And as scaly as a mermaid's tail,
His heart is as cold as ice
And as dark as the night sky,
There are poisonous spikes going down his back,
Of course, it is very black.

Elissa Cummings (10)
Townhill Primary School, Townhill

The Town Journey

The monster goes to Parliament
And then ends up in the town,
Then he meets the queen
And the queen gives him a crown.

Over the party mountain
The monster goes to sleep,
Then he goes to a field
And then he sees a sheep.

That is the end of his journey,
He was left, now he's lonely,
His life ended up as trash,
He really needs some cash!

Jay Paterson (10)
Townhill Primary School, Townhill

Sparkie The Nice Monster

Sparkie is a nice monster
Just as nice as a flower,
His eyes are blue, just like the sky,
His hair is fluffy, just like a cat,
His teeth are sharp like a shark,
His nails will leave a mark!
Just yesterday, his sister called him,
Hooray!
He no longer has to live with a dog in the trash,
Sparkie is happy, just like a monkey,
I'm happy for Sparkie,
Hooray!

Carlo Bosshardt (9)
Townhill Primary School, Townhill

The Monster In The Street

It was fully pitch-black,
In the middle of the night,
The stars were shining thoroughly,
The moon was shining bright.

Just down the street,
In the middle of the road,
There was a fluffy monster
Out in the dark and cold.

He looked like he was freezing,
He looked like he was cold,
He looked as still as can be
In the middle of Lochview Road.

Eden Murray (10)
Townhill Primary School, Townhill

My Little Monster

My little monster,
As hairy as can be,
When I ask to pet it,
It asks to pet me!

I try to teach it how to eat,
But it thinks my feet are a treat!

"Where do you come from?"
I say with a smile,
"I come from a planet
Oh so very vile!"

Now, my monster stays with me
And, really, he's a mini-me!

Sarah Elliott (10)
Townhill Primary School, Townhill

The Scary Night

As the night sky came to an end,
A monster came and jumped
Into the lava of a volcano.

Ten minutes later, it all erupted
All over the houses under it.

His teeth were as sharp as knives
And he was wise,
He was as green as the Grinch
And he smelt like rotten banana and beef.

He died by falling off the volcano.

Harris Penman (10)
Townhill Primary School, Townhill

My Monster Friend

This is my monster friend,
She is very sweet,
Lover of honey,
Lover of sweets,

Eyes of stars sparkling
In the night sky,
Teeth as sharp as bread knives,
But doesn't ever bite,
As cute as Kool-Aid,

She likes to go on walks,
Seems as if she is scary
But really is not.

Abigail Rintoul (11)
Townhill Primary School, Townhill

Fluffy Monsters!

I am a big, fluffy monster,
I have a heart of gold,
Just like lovely monsters,
A diamond crown to feel like a queen,
Cotton candy eyes with jaguar teeth,
Me, you, huge, fluffy monster,
Whatever the weather,
I am a huge, fluffy monster!

Chanelle Aspey (10)
Townhill Primary School, Townhill

The Ugly Monster

He's spotty and he is naughty,
He did the potty, won the lottery
And screamed twice.

He went to the spa, got a car,
He is angry like Fred,
He's angry like a bull.
He has sharp teeth like knives.

Arran Mitchell (11)
Townhill Primary School, Townhill

Fang

Don't mess with the monster that's called Fang
If you go near him he'll make a loud bang
From a clear glass he drinks vampire blood
Not long after that he rolls in the mud
Fang the monster is really very scary
And the small piece of hair on his head is hairy
The monster has big, scary, green eyes
Because of them, everyone hears little children's cries
When people go near him they tremble with fear
And if he comes closer they will shed a tear
His two white fangs are as sharp as a claw
He doesn't go by any rules and always breaks the law
Everybody looks for him, he's very very rare
And if anybody finds him it's impossible not to stare
If anyone sees him they will get really scared
Also, if their friends knew about it they would for sure have cared.

Abbi Foubister (10)
Turriff Primary School, Turriff

Angelic Amythest

This is Amethyst,
She is oh-so-cute and fluffy
And not huffy or puffy
Although she is kind and cute
You won't want to get in a dispute
For her horns are as tough as steel
And if she's hungry you might be her meal

If you see her in your dreams
You will see her beautiful eyes gleam
So if you see her don't be rude
Just try to be her friend
Because we can conclude if you're rude
You may come to an end

She has angel wings softer than a feather
You can see her fly high if it's good weather
Even though she wants to swoop in and save the day
She can't seem to stop her monstrous ways

In some ways she's angelic
But in others she is demonic

Her personality is twisted
And her future is a bit misted
So we recommend if she comes to say hey
That you ask her to join in and play.

Nevis Ross (11)
Turriff Primary School, Turriff

Frightening But Friendly

Frightening Fin is fluffier than a fleece,
But he has razor-sharp teeth.
He loves to play and loves to eat,
But oh please! Don't smell his feet!

His eyes are almost as big as his giant mouth,
And his tail is much longer than a water spout.
He has a small button nose and pale fur,
And he has a grey belly and cat-like ears.

He's as fast as the Flash,
But when it comes to food
He can't make it last.
Well, that's because he eats it real fast.

Even though he may sound scary,
Good thing he doesn't eat fairies.
That's because he feels too scary,
But that doesn't stop him eating steak and chicken like his sister, Mary.

So even though he's scary,
He's learnt his lesson

Not to eat little kids.
Otherwise, it makes him the opposite of a good fairy.

Zara McKenzie (10)
Turriff Primary School, Turriff

Thunder Is Out

He woke up from his cave,
He wanted to play.
He asked the kids
But they said, "Go away!

You're hairy!
We only like the tooth fairy!"
"I promise I won't bite,
I only eat dairy."

"You said that last time
But you ate Harry."
"I spat him out
Just like Barry."

"You can't play.
You're far too tiny
And when you're scared
You're a bit slimy.

You float on a cloud
And we walk on the ground.

You are just a bit scary."
"But I'm not as scary as Monster Mary.

I'll go back to my cave,
Sad without a dad."
"Come on over, we're bored,
We'd rather play than be sad."

Jay Dow (11)

Turriff Primary School, Turriff

The Snuggle Monster

This is Snuggles, she's a really friendly monster
Unlike a pinching, snipping lobster
She's super fluffy like clouds in the sky
And as sweet as a nice cherry pie.

She doesn't come out much, she's very rare
You would not see her at a funfair
She eats and eats and eats and eats
Her favourite food is nice chewy sweets.

The tail of Snuggles is the size of a snake
It twists and turns just like a lake
You would be stunned by the fluff on her legs
Her cute little toes, the size of pegs.

You wouldn't believe the size of her one eye
She can jump and jump but cannot fly
So that is Snuggles the hungry fluff
You could stroke her for weeks on end but that would never be enough!

Eilidh Paterson (11)
Turriff Primary School, Turriff

The Closet Monster

F luffy I am
L ovely and playful
U s monsters just want some friends
F un is not what it's like
F un is not a thing to us!

T he only thing we want to do is play
H elp us today
E veryone deserves a chance!

M onsters have to sit around and not be seen
O h, if you wanted to know what I look like here it is
N atural teal and purple horns come out of my head
S o much coloured fluff is on me
T remendous tail I have, swish swoosh it goes
E ven if you don't have a tail you're perfect
R emember, monsters are the best!

Dani Morrison (11)
Turriff Primary School, Turriff

Snakeificus Monsterificus

The Snakeificus Monsterificus
With its dragon-like wings
It swoops and soars up and down
Before your clock rings

Its slender snake body doesn't make a sound
So when it sneaks in your room
It will unexpectedly pound

With its sharp, deadly teeth
It bites and scratches you
To see if you are beef
But if you make it a cake
It will use its sharp horns to eat the cake whole
But when it does the ground will begin to shake

But this creature has one eye
Which doesn't look appealing
Like a sweet sweet pie

But the thing that makes it stand out is its luminous spots
So when it's sneaking down the street
It looks like flashing dots.

Sandy McKenzie (10)
Turriff Primary School, Turriff

The Huge Fox At KFC

Argh, he's coming help!
Quick, put up the shield.
It's big, it's bad,
There is chicken to be had.

His daunting moustache on a wrinkly face,
At Kentucky Fried Chicken he is a disgrace.
"Quick, barricade the doors. Close the windows."
Thump, thump, thump! His heft is near though.

He trips on a toilet factory and his arm hits an automobile.
Bang! Crash! Wallop! Out comes its wheel.
Boom! His bulk is getting closer,
Then he stops and bends over.

Smash, bang, crash! KFC is no more.
The one thing left standing is the door.

Louis James Alexander (11)
Turriff Primary School, Turriff

The Story Behind Fred

Freckle-Face Fred
He intercepts your dreams
Putting you quickly asleep
He is very good with schemes
But he is terrible with action
So he assembled a contraption
Then you wake up unable to scream
Because he scares you in your dreams
He grabs you with his 'reemes'
And then he jumps, *whoosh,*
All the way to his cave
Where he has a quick rave
Before eating hi... Ow! I have a stave
He returned the boy because he is sad
He then vows to never eat humans again
Only dairy with his mother Mary
He then became a fairy and he loves it!

Dean Murdoch (11)
Turriff Primary School, Turriff

Glitter Cake

Glitter glitter is everywhere
Glitter glitter is in your hair
Sparklebum is everywhere
Sparklebum is in the air
Fluttering and flying in your house
Watching and waiting for a spouse

She is fluffy and hungry, hungry for glitter
Even better, hungry for you!
She is as hungry as a giant elephant

But she finds a cake shop and sees a massive sparkly cake
She makes herself angry and knocks down the door
Boom!
The door lands on the floor with a clatter
She takes the cake and flies away.
No harm done.

Leah McIntosh (10)
Turriff Primary School, Turriff

Cute, Scary Devil

If you take an angel monster and a devil monster
It makes a huge monster
That is very hungry for children

If you ever come in contact with
Cute Scary Devil
Don't be fooled
It will gobble you up
Gobble! Gobble! Gobble!

In the night when you sleep
He comes in your room
And looks down at you
And then eats you up!

He steals your clothes in his pouch
Sews them together
And wears them to work

Now you know that if you come in contact with
Cute Scary Devil, run and go!

Kelsie Mair (10)
Turriff Primary School, Turriff

Shape-Shifter Joe

Shape-Shifter Joe can turn into anything he wants
He can turn into anything that grunts
He has very big horns
In his original form
So beware, his is coming to get you
Shape-Shifter Joe has one single tooth
He can bite you very hard that you will go, "Oof!"
That tooth is on him all the time
In his original form
So beware, he is coming to get you
He is as stupid as a monkey
But if he wasn't stupid he would be able to get the key
He is only stupid
In his original form
So beware, he is coming for you.

Jamie Murray (11)
Turriff Primary School, Turriff

Fuzzball

A tiny fuzzy monster,
With big blue eyes.
Try to sleep at night,
Then you'll hear the monster's cries.

He's very purple and fluffy,
But at the same time very stuffy.
He lives in the mountain,
And smashes every fountain.

He's like a fire-breathing dragon,
And steals stuff from wagons.
His tummy rumbles like thunder,
But smells like a ball of blunder.

He's as fuzzy as a peach,
And loves to go to the beach.
He's as fast as a cheetah,
He will always beat ya.

Leah Robertson (11)
Turriff Primary School, Turriff

Speedy

Speedy is tiny
He's not a needy monster
When he's going by, be wary
Of his *boom!*
Like a big bass drum

Speedy gets quite hungry
So he runs to Hungary
To get some good curry
But if the curry is too hot
He's out like a speeding bullet

He also sheds his fur
In a very quick manner
Speedy does it so quick
It's faster than a supernova
But don't quiver in fear

So if you see him
Beware, that he's a speedy monster
And might make your ears ring.

Hugh Paterson (11)
Turriff Primary School, Turriff

Crumplet

She's as hungry as a monster
As fluffy as a puppy
But without she's vicious
And she is always acting suspicious

Crumplet is always outgoing
And never stops growing
She never gives up even if she's short

She is always going crazy
That's her favourite thing to do
Everybody thinks she is very lazy
Which is definitely not true

Why doesn't she just be lazy
Like everyone else is?
No, she wouldn't do that, she is too crazy
Well, now we know all about Crumplet.

Grace Macdonald (11)
Turriff Primary School, Turriff

Zig's Life As A Monster

This is Zig the little monster,
He lives his life with nothing but torture.
Hide, people! Hide!
There are monsters in town and they're going to bite!
Zig runs and tries to hide
But everybody screams when he's in sight.
Zig might seem like the best,
But he's definitely the odd one out from the rest.
He runs as fast as a cheetah,
At the beginning of a race he'll say, "I'll beat ya!"
Zig's getting tired now, it's time for bed,
"Goodnight!" he says to his father, Ted.

Victoria Strachan (11)
Turriff Primary School, Turriff

Sid, The Slimy Savarian

When you are asleep at night,
Don't wake up because you'll get a fright.

If your bedroom's clean, no need to worry,
If not, clean it quick, come on, go, hurry!

Or...

Sid the slimy Savarian will come out from under your bed,
He'll take you clothes, he'll show you affection.

He stores our clothes in a pouch,
If he's super hungry he will eat your couch.

So don't say I haven't warned you because I have,
Because Sid the slimy Savarian will get sad.

Evie Acklaw (11)
Turriff Primary School, Turriff

Elvis

Elvis is very clumsy,
He can accidentally eat you while you are asleep.

He has a big purple eye,
If you see him he will actually make you cry.

He's as clumsy as a lion without legs,
He will come and eat you if you don't give him some bread.

When he is walking down the street with no food to eat,
He walks past the bakers
Boom! Goes the door with a clatter and a beat.

Oh, dear friendly monster, what a wonderful thing
Oh, dear friendly monster, I wish you could sing!

Lois Beaton (11)
Turriff Primary School, Turriff

Chad, The Friendly Fool

He's soft like a house cat,
You can even use his fur for a house mat.

He's got three ears but a lot of fears.
His body is kind of human-like
And he doesn't have a lot of spikes.

He wants to be your friend and not a fiend.

He's as happy as someone who just won the World Cup,
And he always likes to ask his friends, "What's up?"
But when he's hungry his stomach rumbles like a rhino running, it's truly stunning.
This is Chad,
He never gets mad.

Safwan Misbah Chowdhury (11)
Turriff Primary School, Turriff

Diva The Monster's Poem!

Like a fluffy blanket, Diva is soft
She's as crazy as a dog after its treat
And is as tiny as a mouse that lives in your loft
Her hair is as silky as a cat's fur on a hot day

Her teeth are as sharp as razors
But her horns are like needles
Diva's eye is as red as a laser
And her sense of smell is way better than yours

Diva is four, she loves to make you smile
Her birthday is the 13th of October
Although she might be scary,
She wants to be your friend.

Charley Nicole Ritchie (11)
Turriff Primary School, Turriff

Freaky Steve

He's as creepy as Chucky
He's as mechanical as Terminator
He can shape-shift like the Viking god Loki
Steve is huge, Steve is freaky
He's as loud as a foghorn
His snake fingers hiss like a pipe releasing gas
His teeth chomp like the jaws of a car crusher
Steve is huge, Steve is freaky
Steve has thin slimy anacondas for fingers to help him climb
He has horns of a bull, he has nine
Body of a robot to tell him the time
Steve is huge, Steve is freaky.

Cameron Archibald (11)
Turriff Primary School, Turriff

Dave The Monster

A scary monster who is a slimy blob
You mess with him, he'll turn you into slippery slob.
As heavy as a bowling ball,
You may catch him in the mall.

Thunderously, he can magnetically pull his enemies to him,
He will bang your limb.
He is as dark as the night sky,
Randomly he goes around thinking he can fly!

His favourite food is human,
He likes the blood, it's very good!
He likes the meat,
He considers it a treat!

Archie Hart (11)
Turriff Primary School, Turriff

Flufflls The Monster

Flufflls is very fluffy,
Unlike his friend, Scruffy.
Flufflls is very athletic,
Sadly, his friends are pathetic.

Flufflls is as cuddly as a teddy bear,
And he's always there to care.
He's so big it's hard not to stare,
People love him so much because he's so rare.

Sadly, Flufflls lives so far away,
To get to his house you have to walk for a day.
Everyone loves Flufflls but sadly he passed away.

Innes Milne (11)
Turriff Primary School, Turriff

Bubbles

Bubbles is a fluffy, friendly giant
But sometimes he can be a tyrant
He goes into houses and steals their food
Some people say he's really quite rude
He'll munch on his snacks all through the night
And if people spot him they will get a fright
But apart from that, Bubbles is really kind
Oh, I forgot to mention that he's blind
He can't see that he's wrong
This rhyme is kind of like a song.

Eilidh Jayne Gerrard (11)
Turriff Primary School, Turriff

Sweet But Psycho

He is as fluffy as a kitten,
And has hands like mittens.

Rips your skin,
Without a pin.

His eyes as big as a clock face,
And leaves without a trace.

His name is Gibble-Gobble,
And he sometimes does a little wobble.

He is quite sneaky,
But he looks a bit peaky.

Make sure you don't make a peep,
Or he will be there when you're asleep.

Tazmin Lyon Raffan (11)
Turriff Primary School, Turriff

The Scared Pike

Come out, Pike. Come out, Pike.
Monsters want to come and fight
You better run, you better hide
They're hungry, they're grumpy
And coming to eat your meat
Take your treats, take your meats
And run away into the murky night
They're hungry, they're grumpy
And want to feast on a treat
That is you
Pike is sneaky but meek
They're hungry, they're grumpy.

Harvey Ross (11)
Turriff Primary School, Turriff

A Bat Called Larry

Larry is not a normal bat
He's fast, smart and evil
He creeps and crawls and flies at night
His eyes flash like lightning
It is very frightening
He might be cute and fluffy
But he still might bite
His only weakness is the light
So watch all night because
He might be waiting for
Your light to go out so
Goodbye and good luck!

Fraser Mann (11)
Turriff Primary School, Turriff

The Big, Friendly Monster

He is so furry
It looks like he was dragged out of a holly bush backwards.
He meets me down on this deck
He knocks on the door which makes a peck
He is a big friendly thing
But he can flip with a bing
So don't go on his bad side
Or you will end up on the tide
Don't forget to be kind
Because he will actually mind.

Richie Renwick (11)
Turriff Primary School, Turriff

Dave

Dave is small, as small as a doll
He is not as skinny as one
Dave is colourful as a rainbow
Light blue and yellow
Mum and dad is friendly
And he is too
He scares his big brother with a boo
He plays tag with his friend
Having fun till the day ends.

Jack Rutherford (11)
Turriff Primary School, Turriff

Helppy

Helppy will go to sleep at 10pm
And wake up at 8am
To help people
He will look around for anyone who needs help
Then he will go and fly to them
Help them and never lets them down
Then he goes somewhere else to help other people.

Hamish Wilson (11)
Turriff Primary School, Turriff

The Small Splash

He will run under your door
Jump on your bed and eat your cookies
Take your socks and hide them
Make a mess and tell your mum
You'll wake and you'll see a king ant
When he jumps he makes a splash.

Grajan Loba (11)
Turriff Primary School, Turriff

Brockle

Brockle is old and small
Scary and green
He'll definitely make you scream.
He can shape-shift,
Maybe into you!
Or maybe something smelly
Which could just be a poo.

Brodie Laing (11)
Turriff Primary School, Turriff

Cloudy

Cloudy is a friendly boy
People call him a toy

When you go to sleep
He will give you a peep
He will give you a cuddle.

Logan Douglas (11)
Turriff Primary School, Turriff

Mr Yeti

A huge yeti
Who loves confetti
And he eats spaghetti
His name is Mike
And he's fat and sweaty.

Luke Gardiner (11)
Turriff Primary School, Turriff

YOUNG WRITERS INFORMATION

We hope you have enjoyed reading this book – and that you will continue to in the coming years.

If you're a young writer who enjoys reading and creative writing, or the parent of an enthusiastic poet or story writer, do visit our website **www.youngwriters.co.uk**. Here you will find free competitions, workshops and games, as well as recommended reads, a poetry glossary and our blog. There's lots to keep budding writers motivated to write!

If you would like to order further copies of this book, or any of our other titles, then please give us a call or order via your online account.

Young Writers
Remus House
Coltsfoot Drive
Peterborough
PE2 9BF
(01733) 890066
info@youngwriters.co.uk

Join in the conversation!
Tips, news, giveaways and much more!

YoungWritersUK @YoungWritersCW